A Robbie Reader

Meet Our New Student From

ISRAEL

Laya Saul

Mitchell Lane
PUBLISHERS

P.O. Box 196
Hockessin, Delaware 19707
Visit us on the web: www.mitchelllane.com
Comments? email us: mitchelllane@mitchelllane.com

Meet Our New Student From

Australia • China • Colombia • Great Britain • Haiti • **Israel** • Korea • Malaysia • Mexico • New Zealand • Nigeria • Tanzania

PUBLISHER'S NOTE: The facts on which the story in this book is based have been thoroughly researched. Documentation of such research can be found on page 44. While every possible effort has been made to ensure accuracy, the publisher will not assume liability for damages caused by inaccuracies in the data, and makes no warranty on the accuracy of the information contained herein.

To reflect current usage, we have chosen to use the secular era designations BCE ("before the common era") and CE ("of the common era") instead of the traditional designations BC ("before Christ") and AD (*anno Domini*, "in the year of the Lord").

Library of Congress Cataloging-in-Publication Data
Saul, Laya.
Meet our new student from Israel / by Laya Saul.
 p. cm. — (A Robbie reader)
Includes bibliographical references and index.
ISBN 978-1-58415-651-2 (library bound)
 1.Israel—Juvenile literature.I. Title.
DS118.S3144 2009
956.94—dc22
2008002277

Printing 1 2 3 4 5 6 7 8 9

PLB

CONTENTS

Israel

Sunbathers enjoy the
beach at Caesarea
Palaestina, a city built
by Herod the Great about
25–13 BCE. Like many
places in Israel, the city
blends modern life with
ancient history.

New Kid Alert!

Chapter 1

"New kid alert, new kid alert!" Mr. Louth announced. I stopped gazing out the window at the tall Rocky Mountains and looked at our teacher. A new kid is big news because we always have a party when someone joins our class.

"Who is it?" Ben called out.

"Where's the new kid from?" Sarah squealed. Naomi elbowed her in the side. "Ow, what'd ya do that for?" Sarah said, but Naomi just put her finger to her mouth and said, "Shhh!"

"Settle down, class." Mr. Louth smiled. "The new student is from Israel."

"Where the heck is that country, anyway?" I asked before I could get my hand in the air. "I've seen it on the news before."

"Well, Stephanie," he answered, "Israel is in the Middle East. We'll have a look at a map, and we'll see what we can learn to help the new student feel

Where in the World

Negev Desert

Lebanon

Syria

Golan Heights

Hermon Mt.

Acre

Haifa • ▲ Mt. Meron

Zippori • Tiberius

Nazareth •

Sea of Galilee

Beit She'an

Mediterranean Sea

Tel Aviv

West Bank

Jerusalem ✪

• Bethlehem

Gaza Strip

Beersheba •

Arad •

Dead Sea

Israel

Jordan

NEGEV

Egypt

Eilat

FACTS ABOUT ISRAEL

Total area: 8,019 square miles (slightly smaller than New Jersey)

Population: 6,426,679 (includes settlers in the West Bank and Golan Heights; 2007 estimate)

Capital City: Jerusalem

Religious Groups: Jewish, Muslim, Arab Christians, other Christian, Druze, unspecified

Languages: Hebrew (official), Arabic is used officially for Arab minority, English is the most commonly used foreign language

Chief Exports: Machinery and equipment, software, cut diamonds, agricultural products, chemicals, textiles and apparel

Monetary Unit: New Israeli Shekel

Forests are not natural to Israel. In 1901 the Jewish National Fund began to repurchase land and pioneers began to hand plant trees. Over 240 million trees have been planted in the land!

welcome. Sound good?" He pulled down a wall map of the world.

We looked for Israel and found a teeny-tiny dot on that map. Israel is such a small country that, on our world map, they had to write the name of it in the sea. How can a whole country be so small? I live in Denver, Colorado, and our state is bigger than Israel. We wanted to know all about that place—the language, the people, and the history. We wanted to learn about the music and food too. I wanted to know about the shopping.

Acre, or 'Akko (AH-koe), on the Mediterranean Sea. The city shows much history, with structures from the Greeks, Romans, Arabs, and Christians.

The official language of Israel is Hebrew. It is the same language in which the Hebrew Bible was written. Hebrew letters are different than the ones in the Roman alphabet, which is used to write English, but here is a list of how to pronounce some Hebrew words and what they mean:

HEBREW	ENGLISH
Shalom	Peace
Mah-neesh-mah	How's it going?
Tove	Good
Ken	Yes
Lo	No
Toh-dah	Thank you
Beh-vah-kah-shah	Please; you're welcome
Boh-kehr tove	Good morning

"The new boy's name is Ziv," Mr. Louth said. "We'll take a day to learn about Israel so that we can help Ziv feel comfortable and welcome when he arrives."

"Hey, maybe we can take some field trips when he comes to show him around Denver!" Ben said. That Ben is such a nice kid. I thought about taking Ziv to the Four Mile House to learn about the pioneers, or Cherry Creek Library, but I wanted to hear more about Israel first, so I didn't say anything.

We got to work right away learning about Israel. We had a ton of questions, and good ol' Mr. Louth was ready with the answers.

Israel

A man prays in the same Hebrew language that was spoken thousands of years ago.

Ancient
Israel

Chapter

The Middle East is a region that spans across parts of Africa and Asia. Israel is in the Asian part of the Middle East, on the eastern coast of the Mediterranean Sea. People have lived in the region for thousands of years.

The history of Israel begins in **ancient** times. Many of the stories from the Bible took place in what is now called Israel. In fact, some of the cities in Israel have the same name today as they did in ancient times. Beit She'an (pronounced *Bet Sheh-AHN*) is one of the cities that are both ancient and modern. The modern part of the city is separate from the ruins of the ancient city.

Archaeologists (ar-kee-AH-luh-jists) have been uncovering ancient sites in Israel for many years. From Arad in the southern desert to Zippori in the north, archaeologists have dug deeper and deeper to learn about the people who lived there. Jerusalem

has many layers of history that have been revealed over thousands of years. Acre ('Akko) is a site from the Christian Crusades.

Anywhere you go in Israel, you can find something from the distant past. All through history, the most powerful people wanted to conquer Israel and the land around it. Each time it was conquered, the culture of that time left a lasting mark—a road, a building, or art of some kind.

The Western Wall in Jerusalem is the last standing wall that surrounded the Jewish Temple, which was destroyed over 2,000 years ago. It is considered the holiest place by the Jewish people.

The ruins of an amphitheater (AM-fih-thee-uh-tur), where people could see a show, still stand in the city of Beit She'an. In ancient times, travelers would stop in Beit She'an for rest, entertainment, and shopping.

Israel's Conquerors	Dates in Power in Israel
Babylonian	586–535 BCE
Persian and Greek Hellenistic	536–142 BCE
Roman	536–142 BCE
Byzantine	313–636 CE
Islamic	636–1099 CE
Christian Crusaders	1099–1291 CE
Mamluk Rule	1291–1516 CE
Ottoman	1517–1917 CE
British	1918–1948 CE

Often when there is a war, the borders of a country change. That has also happened with Israel. (Even today there are a lot of arguments and even wars over who should have what part of the land.) After the Roman Empire conquered the land of Israel in 70 CE, they named it Palestine. It was called Palestine until the modern State of Israel was established in 1948.

Jerusalem is the capital of modern-day Israel, but in ancient times it was also the center of life in the region.

The Hebrew Bible, also called the Torah, is handwritten using the quill of a feather. The entire five books are put together in one long scroll. After a person reads from the scroll, it is lifted into the air. You can see the leather band on the hand (called tefillin) that is used during prayer to "bind" the man to God.

Jerusalem is where King Solomon built the Jewish Temple, and the city was the capital of the Jewish Kingdom.

Solomon's temple was destroyed in 586 BCE when the Syrian Greeks conquered Jerusalem and wanted to destroy the faith of the Jewish nation. Most of the Jews were **exiled** to Babylonia. In 515 BCE, the temple was rebuilt and **rededicated** (ree-DEH-dih-kay-ted). When the Romans invaded in 70 CE, the temple was destroyed for the second time. Most of the Jews fled to other parts of the world. They went to Spain and to some of the Arab countries. This was also an important time in Christian history, since it was during the rule of the Roman Empire that Jesus—who was a Jew—lived and was **crucified** (KROO-sih-fyd) by the Romans. About six hundred years later (in 691 CE), during the Arab rule, the Dome of the Rock (a Muslim **mosque**) was built on the site of the Jewish Temple.

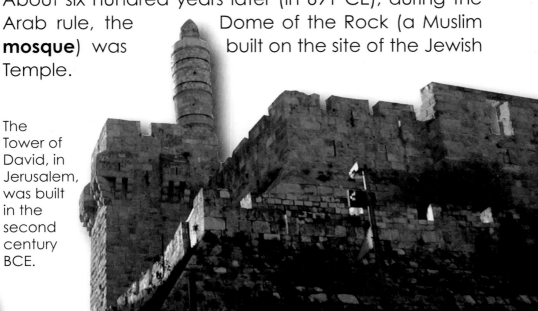

The Tower of David, in Jerusalem, was built in the second century BCE.

The Dome of the Rock is a Muslim place of prayer called a mosque. It is said that the Muslim prophet Muhammad rose to heaven from this spot.

There were other times when the Jewish people had to run away from people who wanted them to change their religion or who even killed them because they were different. They moved to Europe and other countries. Even though most of the Jewish people were forced to leave the land of Israel, it remained very important to them, and they always longed and prayed to return there.

A sacred place for Catholics and Christians is the Basilica of the Annunciation in Nazareth. It is believed that Mary was visited by an angel here and told she would be the mother of Jesus.

The gardens of the
Temple of the Bahaí'í
overlook the modern
port city of Haifa on the
Mediterranean Sea.

Modern
Israel

Chapter

When the Jewish people of modern times returned, sometimes they had to battle disease. Sometimes they had to drain swamps just to have a place to plant a field. Sometimes they had to fight other people who did not want them to return.

During World War II (1939–1945), German leader Adolf Hitler wanted to conquer the world. He set up a cruel system to take the lives of millions of people. In what came to be called the Holocaust, his armies murdered six million Jews. The people who survived felt that the only thing left to do was to go "home" to Israel. The United Nations (UN), where leaders from all over the world meet, voted to let the Jews have some of that land back to make a home for themselves. When that happened in 1948, many Jews who were living in Europe moved to Israel. Most of the Jews who had been living in the Arab countries around Israel moved there also. They returned from many different

places: Africa, Australia, North and South America, Russia, Ethiopia, Iraq, Egypt, France, India, and the United Kingdom.

Not everyone was happy with the UN decision. At the time, the land was under British rule.

Although the UN granted Israel to the Jews, Israelis have had to fight to prevent takeovers from other countries.

The UN tried to create an Arab state at the same time that they created the Jewish state (Israel). However, the Arabs did not accept the idea. In fact, less than a day after Israel was granted independence, Egypt, Syria, Jordan, Lebanon, and Iraq invaded the country. The broken survivors of the Holocaust and farming pioneers had to defend themselves against five armies. Many consider it a miracle that Israel survived and won that War of Independence.

An Israeli soldier stands guard in the Old City of Jerusalem. Soldiers are stationed in many public places around the country to protect the citizens from terrorism.

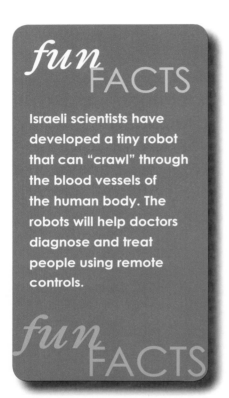

funFACTS

Israeli scientists have developed a tiny robot that can "crawl" through the blood vessels of the human body. The robots will help doctors diagnose and treat people using remote controls.

funFACTS

To this day, the Israelis and Arabs are not at peace. During three other wars, the borders changed as Israel pushed back attacks. Those territories are still in **dispute**. Israel still has to fight terrorism. In Jerusalem, guards stand at bus stops to protect citizens from suicide bombers. Some Arab countries say they want to destroy Israel. Even with these constant challenges, Israel strives to build the country and contribute to the world.

In some places Israelis have had to build big concrete security walls to keep citizens safe from terrorism.

For such a young country, Israel has contributed a lot to the world, including high-tech instant messaging and cell phone technology. It has also made advances in water protection, security, irrigation, and recycling.

In the short time that modern Israel has been a state, a lot has happened. The country has grown in many ways from the days of draining swamps and planting trees. Today, Israel hosts a big international airport. It has universities and hospitals. The people of Israel have put their small country on the map as a world leader in technology, medicine, and sciences.

Visitors come from around the world to pray at the Western Wall in Jerusalem. Tucked between the stones are prayers that are handwritten on small notes.

Built on
Faith

Chapter **4**

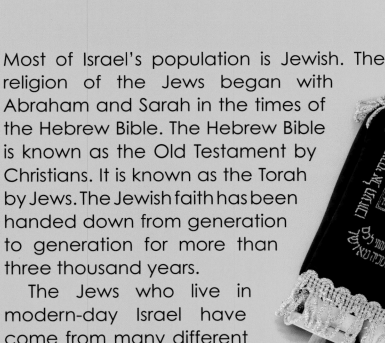

Most of Israel's population is Jewish. The religion of the Jews began with Abraham and Sarah in the times of the Hebrew Bible. The Hebrew Bible is known as the Old Testament by Christians. It is known as the Torah by Jews. The Jewish faith has been handed down from generation to generation for more than three thousand years.

The Jews who live in modern-day Israel have come from many different lands around the world. Each group of Jews brings something from the land in which they lived: food, culture, art, or music. No matter where in the

Torah

world they have lived, they all celebrate the same holidays and say the same prayers in the ancient Hebrew language.

Many Jewish men wear a head covering called a **kippah**, or yarmulke, to remind them that God is always above them. Religious Jewish men also wear tzitzit. These are tassels tied in special knots to each corner of a four-cornered garment. The tzitzit serve to remind the wearer to keep the laws of the Torah. Religious Jewish men and women follow laws of **modesty.**

Jews also follow laws from the Bible about the foods they can eat. They may eat only animals that have split hooves and chew their cud, such as cows or sheep. They may not eat meat and dairy at the same meal. These laws about food are called *kashrut* ("**kosher**" in English). Even in the United States, some food packages are printed with a symbol that lets customers know the food is kosher.

Kippah

Holidays

Some of the Jews who live in Israel are very religious, some are not at all, and there is every degree of observance in between. Most everyone celebrates a *lot* of holidays! There is a Jewish holiday almost every single month. Holidays are celebrated according to the ancient Hebrew calendar, which is based on moon cycles instead of the sun. There are also more modern holidays like Independence Day (May 14) and Memorial Day in the spring.

One of the fun holidays is Purim. It celebrates the story of an evil man named Haman who plotted to kill the Jewish people of the Persian Empire. He got the king to agree with his murderous plan. With lots of twists and turns, a Jewish woman named Esther became the

Purim is a favorite holiday, with costumes and lots of fun. Children bring ready-to-eat foods to friends and neighbors, give money to poor people, and share fancy meals with their families.

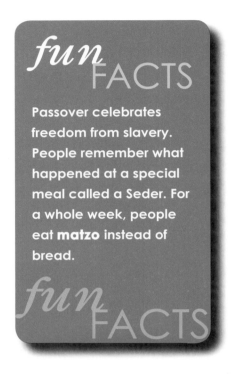

fun FACTS

Passover celebrates freedom from slavery. People remember what happened at a special meal called a Seder. For a whole week, people eat **matzo** instead of bread.

queen. Eventually the bad guy is seen for who he really is, and goodness **triumphs**! The holiday is celebrated by reading the story out loud in **synagogues** (where Jews pray). Whenever Haman's name is spoken, the whole place gets in an uproar, with everyone making a lot of noise and booing him.

Kids and some adults dress up in costumes and act quite silly. Everyone gives baskets of ready-to-eat food to neighbors and friends—even to people with whom they don't get along. It's also a time of giving charity to help poor people.

Other Religions in Israel

In a way, Israel is like a **mosaic** (moh-ZAY-ik) of different cultures and peoples. All citizens of Israel have the right to practice their religion, whatever it may be. There are many Arabs who live in Israel; most of them are Muslim, which means they observe the religion of Islam. Islam also came from Abraham, so in a way, the Jews and the Muslims are related. Some of the Arabs who live in Israel are Christians. Some of the Christians who live in Israel are Armenian, Greek Orthodox, and Russian Orthodox.

The Bahaí'í religion has its main church in Haifa, a city in northern Israel. Druze people (Arabs whose religion is different from Islam) also live in Israel. The Bedouins are a **nomadic** tribe of Arabs. They live in tents in the desert, and many of them herd camels or tend sheep.

Hanukkah, or Chanukah, celebrates the victory of the small Jewish army called the Maccabees against the Seleucids in 165 BCE. The Maccabees freed the Temple and retook Jerusalem. Candles are lit eight days in a row to mark the rededication of the Temple.

In School

The school week in Israel is six days long. Students usually have a half day of school on Friday, and their day off is Saturday—the **Sabbath.** School in Israel is very much like school in the United States. Students have to learn math, history, reading, and writing. They also start learning English in elementary school. In high school they can learn other languages if they want. They do art projects, and some schools teach how to play musical instruments. Kids in Israel love to

Boys from a religious school are taking a break. In many religious schools, boys and girls learn separately.

play during recess. They always have a break in the morning at ten o'clock, when they eat sandwiches brought from home. In the afternoon when they get home from school, they eat a big hot meal, kind of like dinnertime in the United States. Their dinner is a light meal, kind of like the American lunch.

Israeli Army

Israel is always under the threat of war from surrounding Arab countries, so the army must always be ready to fight. After they graduate from high school, all young men and women are called to serve in the Israeli Army. Women were not allowed in combat units after the War for Independence, but that changed in the late 1990s. The first female fighter pilot graduated in 2001. Instead of army service, young religious women may choose to do a year of National Service. That might involve helping in a hospital or a school program.

Young men serve for three years, and women for less than two. In addition to the required service, Israeli men continue to serve in the reserves into their early fifties. That means that if a war starts, Israel can have hundreds of thousands of soldiers ready within hours.

Climate

The climate in Israel is temperate, which means not too hot and not too cold. Mostly the weather is sunny and warm. A large part of Israel is hot, dry desert. There are beaches in Israel, and also mountains. A lot of people compare the climate to that in California. In fact, many of the plants that grow in Israel, such as grapes, olives, oranges, and avocados, also grow in California.

About half of Israel is the Negev desert in the south. It is not like some deserts that are all sand. The Negev is mostly rocks and dirt. Israeli cities and even farms are built on the desert.

People like to ski at Hermon Mountain resort in northern Israel. While there is snow on the mountain, southern Israel is a desert called the Negev.

Famous People of Israel

You might recognize these famous Israelis: Actress Natalie Portman played the role of Queen Amidala in the *Star Wars* movies. The voice of Yocheved from Disney's *Prince of Egypt* is Ofra Haza, who was Israeli. Israeli Gal Fridman won an Olympic gold medal for windsurfing. Golda Meir, a former prime minister of Israel, was the world's third elected woman leader.

Itzhak Perlman is a world-class violinist. Colonel Ilan Ramon was an astronaut who lost his life on the Space Shuttle *Columbia*.

Free Time
Israel is so small that you can drive from the north end of the country all the way to the south in about seven hours. There is a lot to do in Israel for fun. There are nature preserves for hiking, beaches for water sports, and trails to go horseback riding. There are museums of science, history, and art. There are zoos and lots of ancient ruins of historical sites.

Although people can swim in it, the Dead Sea has so much salt that nothing can live in it, not a fish or a plant. It is very dense from all that salt, so people who go in will float.

Scarves are displayed for sale at the Shuk Ha'Carmel in Tel Aviv. This open-air market extends along many streets in Tel Aviv, selling everything from hats to crafts to fish, fruits, nuts, and spices. Vendors call out about their products and prices to help attract customers.

Sports are big in Israel. When they say "football" in Hebrew, they mean soccer. There are malls in Israel too. Sometimes people shop in a **shuk** (SHOOK). A *shuk* is an open marketplace that is like a farmers' market, where **vendors** sell produce, clothes, jewelry, candy, and toys. There are movie theaters where Israelis see the same movies that people in the United States see. The TV stations in Israel have programs in Hebrew, Arabic, Russian, English, Spanish, and French.

Ziv rests on a mosaic
decoration in a park
in Tiberius.

Ziv
Arrives

Chapter

We were all squirming around in our seats before our new classmate from Israel, Ziv, arrived. He looked nervous as he walked through the door. We all started to say the words we had learned in Hebrew: *"Shalom! Mah-neesh-mah?"* (Hello! What's up?) Then he gave us a huge grin! Mr. Louth stood next to Ziv and said, "Class, meet Ziv, our new student from Israel."

"Boh-kehr tove," called out Sarah.

"Good morning!" Ziv answered in English, and his smile got bigger still. "Nice to meet you." His eyes darted around the room at each one of us.

Mr. Louth asked him to tell us a little bit about himself. Ziv had an accent, but we could understand him just fine. "I moved here from a town in northern Israel called Tiberius. My father is a doctor, and we will live in Denver for two years while my father works at the hospital."

"What's it like in Tiberius?" asked Naomi.

"Well, there are mountains where I am from, but they are not as big as the Rockies. Tiberius is a town that is next to the Kineret. In English you call it something different . . . eh . . ."

He looked at Mr. Louth, who filled in for him. "When we look at a map in English, it's called the Sea of Galilee."

"Yes," Ziv said, relieved. "It is very beautiful and a lot of fun too. Lots of people like to go out on boats, or have picnics by the shore."

Ben raised his hand, then said, "Wow, I didn't think you'd speak English."

"I learned to speak in school." Ziv smiled. "But I learned a lot from movies. I love movies."

Ben grinned now. "Hey, me too!".

For Ziv's party, we prepared hummus, a kind of dip that you can eat with raw vegetables or wedges of pita bread.

The Star of David (also known as the Shield of David) is made up of two triangles on top of each other: One points up and the other points down. The Star of David shows that the Jewish people rely on God as their greatest protection from all directions: up, down, north, east, south, and west. The Star of David is in the center of the Israeli flag.

Ziv tries to decide which candies to buy at a shuk.

The new student, Ziv, walks in his neighborhood in Tiberius. The electrical boxes there were painted by different artists.

Then it was time for crafts. We made a nameplate mosaic using little square stones.

I asked Ziv about the shopping. He told me that there are lots of malls in Israel. He also told me his favorite thing to do was to go to the *shuk* with his friends and stock up on candy. I guess some things are the same for all kids, no matter where they're from!

How To Make
Hummus

Instructions

1. Drain the liquid from the garbanzo beans into a bowl and save.

2. Blend the beans and garlic in a blender with the lemon juice, tahini, and 2 tablespoons of olive oil.

3. Add small amounts of the liquid from the can of beans until the hummus is smooth and creamy.

4. Spread the dip on a plate and drizzle a little bit of olive oil on top. Sprinkle with paprika or parsley to make it pretty. You can also decorate it with a few whole beans.

5. Serve with wedges (triangles) of pita bread for dipping. It also goes well with cut raw veggies, such as cauliflower, cucumbers, bell peppers, and carrots.

Things You Will Need

An adult
Knife
Cutting Board
Blender
Can opener
Bowl
Measuring cup
Measuring spoons
Plate

Ingredients

2 15-ounce cans of garbanzo beans (also known as chick peas)

2 cloves fresh garlic OR 2 teaspoons garlic powder

¼ cup lemon juice

¼ cup tahini paste (you can buy this at a health food store)

Olive oil

Paprika or parsley (optional)

Make Your Own
Mosaic

You Will Need

Pencil

Paper

Construction Paper, Felt, Plastic, or Stone

Glue

Cardboard

There are many mosaics in Israel. They are found on buildings and even on a type of shoe. The method dates from the time of the Byzantine (BIH-zin-teen) Empire.

This ancient mosaic shows a seven-branched menorah, a lulav (palm branch), and a shofar (ram's-horn trumpet). In addition it has a Hebrew inscription: *Shalom al yisrael*, "Peace upon Israel."

Instructions for Making A Mosaic

1 Draw a design for a mosaic on a piece of paper. You can print your name or any other design you like.

2 Once you know the design you want, draw it onto a base of cardboard or wood.

3 Glue squares of paper, felt, or stone into place to form the pattern or letters with one color. Then fill in the spaces all around them with squares of another color. Use colors that contrast (light and dark, or complementary colors) so that your design will stand out.

Further Reading

Books

Fontes, Justine, and Ron Fontes. *Israel A to Z*. New York: Children's Press, 2004.

Hintz, Martin. Israel: *Enchantment of the World*. Revised Edition. New York: Children's Press, 2006.

Rivlin, Lilly. *Welcome to Israel!* Springfield, New Jersey: Behrman House Publishing, 2000.

Sofer, Barbara. *Ilan Ramon: Israel's Space Hero*. Minneapolis: Kar-Ben Publishing, 2004.

On the Internet

Ahklah: Israel for Children
   http://www.akhlah.com/israel/israel.php

The Kids' Website: Embassy of Israel, Washington, D.C.
   http://www.israelemb.org/kids/

Works Consulted

This book is based on the author's personal experiences in Israel and on the following works:

The Bahá'ís: Does the Bahá'í Faith Have an International Center?
   http://www.Bahaí'í.org/faq/facts/bwc

Good News from Israel
   http://www.newsoftheday.com/

Israel 21C: The Reality of Daily Life in Israel
   http://www.israel21c.org

Israel Defense Forces: Background Information
   http://www.mahal2000.com/information/background/content.htm

Israel Ministry of Foreign Affairs
   http://www.mfa.gov.il/MFA

Further Reading

Israel Science and Technology: Brief History of Israel and the Jewish People
http://www.science.co.il/Israel-history.asp

The Jewish Virtual Library
http://www.jewishvirtuallibrary.org/

Jewish National Fund: "The Recovery of Northern Israel Through a Forest's Eyes," January 3, 2007
http://www.jnf.org/site/PageServer?pagename=Recovery

Simmons, Rabbi Shraga. "Star of David." Aish.com.
http://www.aish.com/literacy/concepts/Star_of_David.asp

Embassy

The Embassy of Israel
3514 International Dr. N.W.
Washington DC 20008
http://www.israelemb.org/
202-364-5500
info@israelemb.org

Glossary

ancient (AIN-chent)—Very, very old.

archaeologists (ar-kee-AH-luh-jists)—People who study history by looking at the old things (like pottery or buildings and other things) they find buried.

crucified (KROO-sih-fyd)—Put to death by having the hands and feet nailed or bound to a cross.

dispute (dis-PYOOT)—An argument or struggle.

empire (EM-pyr)—A major political power with a large territory.

exiled (EK-zyld)—Forced to leave one's home or country.

kippah (KIH-puh)—Head covering used by Jewish men; also called a yarmulke or a skullcap because it fits closely to the top of the head. In Hebrew, it's called a *keepah*.

kosher (KOH-shur)—Following the biblical laws about the foods a Jew is allowed to eat. In Hebrew, the word is *kashrut*.

matzo (MAHT-zuh)—Traditional flat-bread cracker that the Jewish people eat in place of bread during the holiday of Passover.

modesty (MAH-duh-stee)—Dressing and acting in ways that are not too showy or revealing.

mosaic (moh-ZAY-ik)—A decoration made by setting small pieces of tile, stone, or glass on a surface using different colors and patterns.

mosque (MOSK)—A Muslim place of worship.

nomadic (noh-MAD-ik)—Wandering from place to place with no fixed home.

rededicated (ree-DEH-dih-kay-ted)—Performed a second ceremony that gives a regular object purpose, especially a sacred purpose.

Sabbath (SAA-buth)—The seventh day of the week, set apart by biblical teachings as a day of rest from weekday work; for Jews, it begins on Friday at sundown and lasts until Saturday after sunset.

shuk (SHOOK)—An open-air market, like a farmer's market or flea market.

synagogue (SIH-nuh-gog)—A Jewish place of worship.

triumph (TRY-umf)—Victory or success.

vendors (VEN-durs)—People who sell.

Index

ABOUT THE AUTHOR

Laya Saul grew up in California and traveled to Israel for the first time when she was a teenager. After starting a family and living happily in Colorado for ten years, Laya moved with her husband and two kids to live in Israel. She speaks Hebrew (but not as well as her kids!), which is a very interesting language to her. She likes to travel and she also likes to teach. Laya is also known to lots of people as Aunt Laya because she wrote a book for teens (called "*You Don't Have to Learn Everything the Hard Way*) to help them live happier, safer lives.

Laya believes that with constant small acts of love or kindness to each other we can bring about a peaceful world, just like lighting one small candle will chase away the darkness.